THE BLOOD SUCKERS

And Other True Animal Stories

Edited by
Mary Verdick

Illustrated by
John Lawn
and with Photos

Designed by
Les Cone

A Pal Paperback from:
Xerox Education Publications
Middletown, Connecticut 06457

Photo Credits: Pages 7, 11, Wide World; p. 9, A.I.D.; pp. 15, 17, Hal Harrison; p. 26 Marine Studios, Marineland, Fla.; pp. 28, 30, U.S. Navy; p. 33, National Audubon Society; pp. 35, 51, 69, UPI; pp. 41, 64, Cinema Center Films; p. 43, NBC-TV; pp. 77, 81, Grant Heilman; pp. 87, 89, Leonard Lee Rue.

Copyright © 1976 Xerox Corporation. All rights reserved. Publishing, Executive, and Editorial Offices: Xerox Education Publications, 245 Long Hill Road, Middletown, CT 06457. Subscription Offices: Xerox Education Publications, Columbus, OH 43216. Printed in U.S.A. Material in this book may not be reproduced in whole or in part in any form or format without special permission from the publisher.

CONTENTS:

THE BLOOD SUCKERS 5
By Steven Otfinoski

THE ANIMAL THAT DINES ON ITS MATE 13
By Steven Otfinoski

A FRIEND IN THE SEA 24
By Diane Carlson

THE UNCROWNED KING 38
By Diane Carlson

THE ANIMAL THAT BROKE ALL THE RULES 49
By Steven Otfinoski

THE DEADLIEST OF THEM ALL 60
By Diane Carlson

THE PRICE OF HONEY 73
By Diane Carlson

WOLF ON THE RUN 85
By Steven Otfinoski

The Blood Suckers

By Steven Otfinoski

Imagine for a moment that you are an explorer in South America. You and your men are camped out in the back hills. It is morning. You awake in your tent from a peaceful night's sleep.

Suddenly you feel something wet on your toes. Could it be rain? You raise your head and look down the length of your

THE BLOOD SUCKERS

body. Your feet are sticking out of the blanket that covers you. You let out a cry of horror. Your feet are covered with blood. Your blood!

What blood hunter has done this? Dracula? No. Dracula is just a story. This monster is all too real. It is the vampire bat.

But if a bat had bitten your toes, why didn't you wake up? Simple. You didn't feel the bite. The vampire bat's teeth are very tiny. But they are as sharp as a razor. The cut made in your skin was clean and without pain.

You don't have to worry about bleeding to death. The bites on your toes are not deep. The bat broke only small blood vessels. The bleeding is steady but slow.

Vampire bats don't attack like Dracula. They hardly ever bite a human on the neck. They usually go for the feet. That is the part of the body most often left uncovered at night. Sometimes they go for the

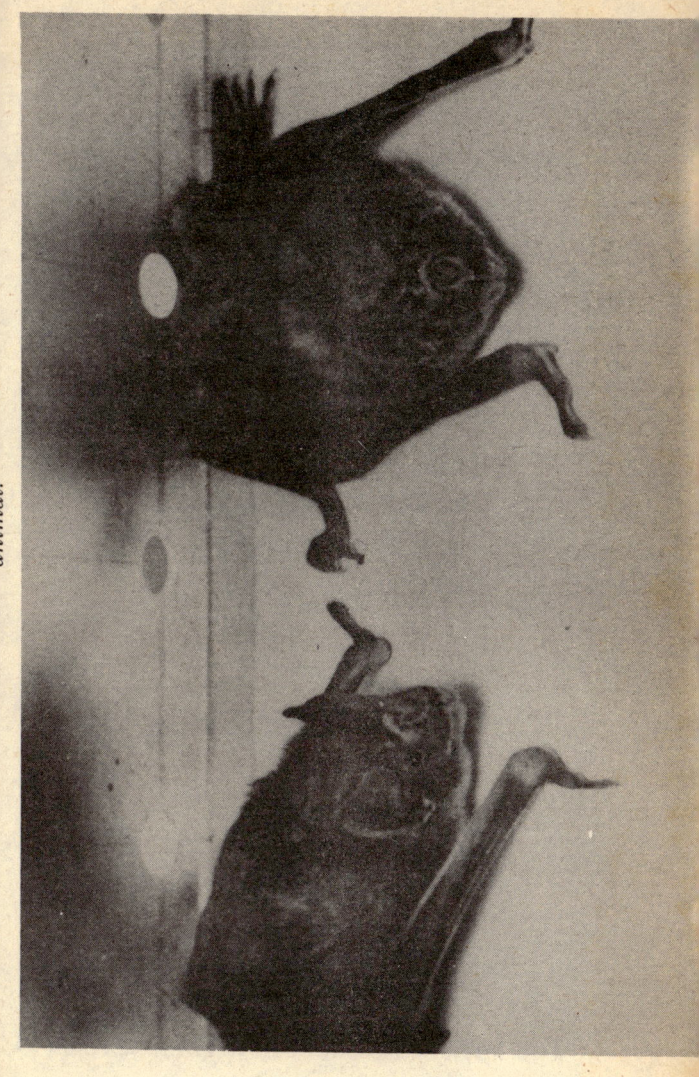

arms and legs too. But only if they are left uncovered.

Although you won't bleed to death, something even worse may happen to you. You may get the disease of rabies. Vampire bats spread rabies just as dogs sometimes do. Sixty people have gotten rabies from vampire bats in the last few years. It is a terrible way to die.

But don't worry too much. The chances are pretty slim you'll even *see* a vampire bat. They only live in Mexico, Central America and South America. They hardly ever attack humans.

They usually live off the blood of horses, chickens, and cattle. About one million head of cattle in South America die each year from rabies caused by vampire bats!

Why do vampire bats drink blood? Why don't they eat insects, fruit, or small fish like other bats?

The answer is, they can't. Their throats

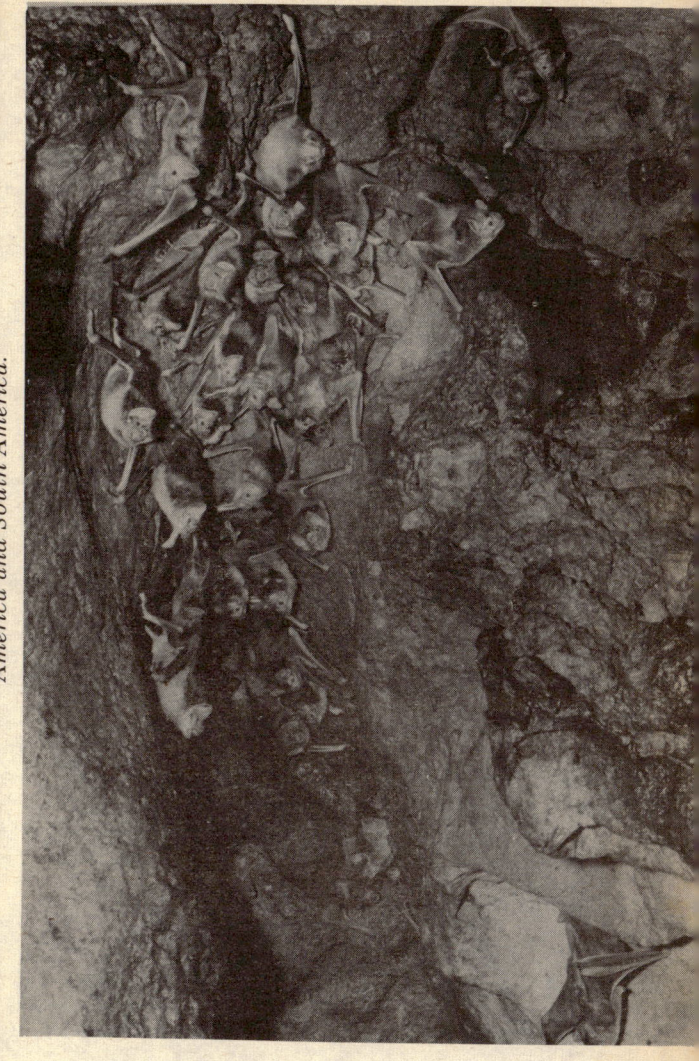

America and South America.

THE BLOOD SUCKERS

are too small. They can't swallow solid food. They must drink blood or die.

You may be surprised to know how vampire bats drink blood. They lap it up with their tongues—like cats drinking milk in a dish.

The vampire bat has only a 3-inch body. When it spreads its wings it is only 8 inches from wing tip to wing tip. It is surprising how much blood this tiny bat drinks! It will lick up blood until its body is a fat, little ball. Then it will spread its wings and fly off to its cave. There it will sleep most of the day.

There are three kinds of vampire bats. Only one kind has been studied by scientists. Several scientists have gone into caves and caught this kind of vampire bat.

Many stories have been told about vampire bats. Some people say they have attacked whole villages. The bats fly around the villagers' heads, like angry bees. Then

The vampire bat has only a 3-inch body. It is only 8 inches from wing tip to wing tip.

THE BLOOD SUCKERS

they dive down and bite the villagers' bodies. The bitten villagers either die from rabies or go mad. That's what the people who tell these stories say anyway.

Some scientists think the vampire bat used to live in other parts of the world. They believe vampire bats may have been in Europe a thousand years ago. Did the story of Dracula grow out of reports about these real vampire bats? No one can say for sure. We only know the vampire bat is still drinking blood today. Real blood.

The Animal That Dines On Its Mate

By Steven Otfinoski

The scorpion is a very strange animal. It breathes through four small lung pockets. These are like the gills of fish. And the scorpion kills its enemies with poison. It grabs the enemy with two large front pincers. Then it paralyzes the enemy with the poison, which the scorpion sends into its enemy through its stinger tail. The poison

THE BLOOD SUCKERS

is so powerful it can kill a man.

But the one most often killed by the scorpion is neither man nor animal. It is the scorpion itself. The story of how all this comes about is not a pretty one. Yet every word of it is true.

Like most animals, scorpions pair off when fully grown. The male scorpion has a funny way of letting a female know he likes her. He stands on his head. This is no easy trick for a scorpion since he has no backbone. His legs are jointed, his body broken up into sections. But somehow he manages.

He leans forward on his pincers and raises the rest of his long body. His tail goes straight up. If the female is interested in him, she'll do the same. The two tails rub together. The stinger ends hook and unhook together again and again. Suddenly, the two scorpions fall apart. They run off in different directions.

his body broken up into sections.

THE BLOOD SUCKERS

The next day they meet again. They take an afternoon walk. The male walks ahead, pulling the female along behind him. She puts up no fight, even though she is bigger than he is.

Finally the male comes to a place he likes. He stops and looks it over carefully. It seems to him like a nice spot to set up house. So he lets one pincer go from the female and begins to dig. His eight legs do the digging. His tail sweeps away the sand that is dug out.

When the hole is deep enough, he enters. He drags his new wife behind him. Here, they spend the night. The next day they are both completely still, locked in each other's arms. They spend the whole day this way.

Night comes again and the male is getting restless. Something tells him he should be on his way. Why? The answer comes quickly.

and looks it over carefully.

THE BLOOD SUCKERS

The female stirs. Slowly, she draws back her tail. Is it possible? Is she going to attack her own husband? The male decides he isn't going to stick around to find out.

He removes his hands from the female. But her combs hold him fast. These combs are found on the lower belly of the scorpion. Their exact purpose is still not known. Right now, though, the teeth of the combs have the male caught. He cannot get away.

Suddenly he feels a sharp stab. The female has struck. Her stinger is deep inside him. Her poison is doing the work. What are his last thoughts as he dies in her arms? Does he wonder, "Why?"

But this story of horror is not yet over. The worst is still to come. The act of killing her husband has left the lady scorpion hungry. She starts to chew slowly on his dead head. When she finishes this, she eats one pincer and then a couple of legs.

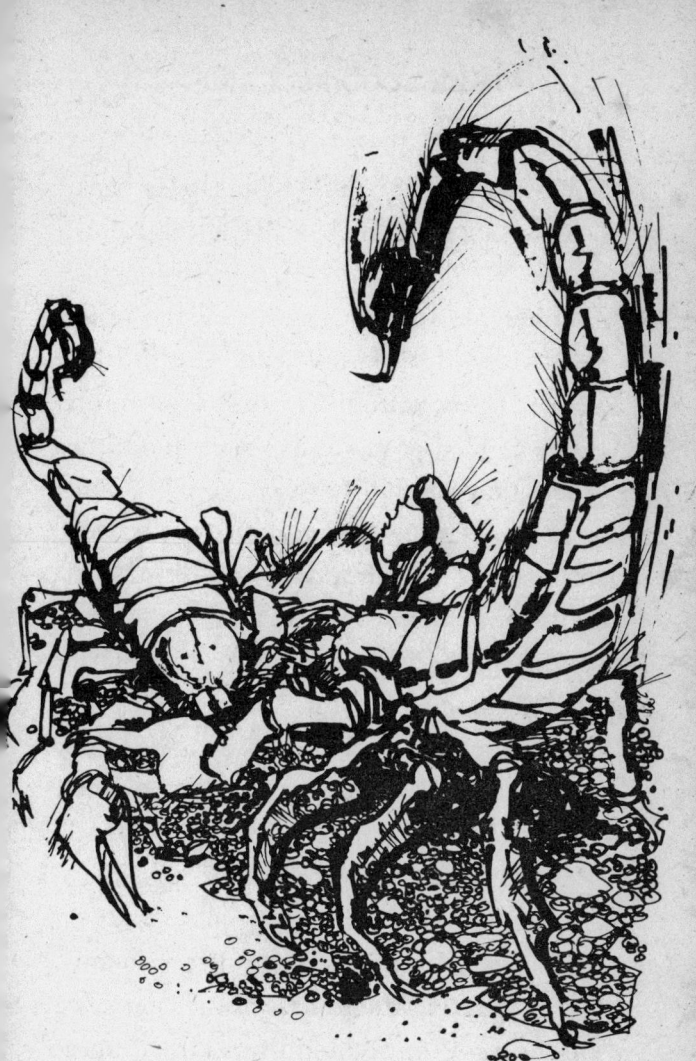

She starts to chew slowly on his dead head.

THE BLOOD SUCKERS

She is now quite full. She settles down next to her dead husband and sleeps for a while.

When morning comes, the lady scorpion goes for a walk. The walk is like the one before, taken with her husband. Only this time she leads. She drags what's left of the male along behind her.

The walk goes on until noon. The lady scorpion seems proud of her dead husband. She shows him off like some prize she has won. Finally, she drops him on the sand. Now it is the ants turn to eat. They move in quickly and finish off what's left of the male. The female moves on—no longer interested. Perhaps she is already thinking about finding another husband.

What could drive any animal to act in such a way? No one is really sure. What we do know is that the female always does the killing. And husband-killing and eating, is not limited to the scorpion.

THE ANIMAL THAT DINES—

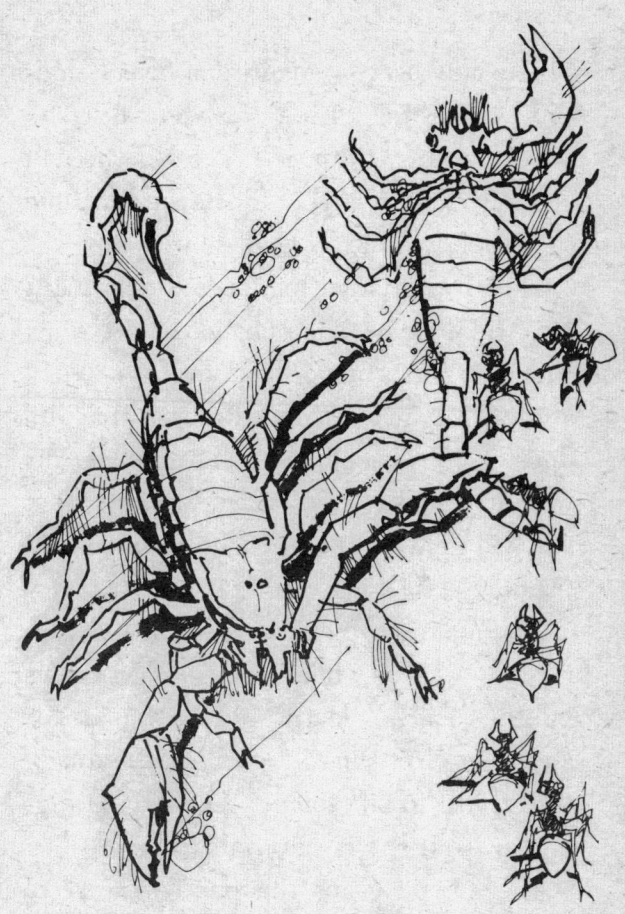

She drags what's left of the male along behind her.

THE BLOOD SUCKERS

The lady praying mantis, an insect, does the same thing to her husband. But she doesn't even wait until he's dead. She will actually eat him alive! Female spiders, like the black widow, also eat their mates.

Does every love match end this way? No. The male has a fair chance to get away. But he must move fast and not hang around. It may seem strange that he doesn't fight back or get the jump on his wife and kill her first. Maybe the fact that she will soon be a mother, holds him back. Or maybe he's just plain dumb.

The male scorpion by nature is a peaceful fellow. You will never see two males fighting to the death—over a female or anything else. When they both see a lady they'd like to take home, they have a tug-of-war. And she is the rope!

Each male grabs the hand nearest to him in one pincer. Then they pull with all their might. If neither gives way after a

THE ANIMAL THAT DINES—

while, the rules change. Each male takes his free pincer and grabs the other's. The three scorpions form a funny kind of chain. They huff and puff and pull and tug. Finally the weaker male gives up. He lets go of the female and hurries away. The winner joins his free pincer to his new wife's, and they take their walk.

What a strange world, where the winner soon turns out to be the loser. And the loser lives to see another day!

A Friend in the Sea

By Diane Carlson

Nervous, worried, the diver waits. The dark waters seem to close in around him. He is far beneath the ocean's surface. He can barely see the dim light from the submarine that brought him down.

Tied to his diving suit is a rope, a guideline. The line is to keep him from drifting too far from the sub and getting lost.

A FRIEND IN THE SEA

"But what if the line breaks?" he asks himself. "What if the plan doesn't work? How long could I stay alive?"

The dark undersea world is no place for a man alone. To breathe, he must bring his air with him in a tank on his back. He can see only a short distance. As a swimmer, he is no match for the sea creatures all around him.

Time is something a diver must keep in mind. "A half hour," he says to himself, "there's only enough air in the tanks for a half hour.

"Well, here goes." He pushes a buzzer strapped to his wrist.

Suddenly a huge gray form appears ahead of him. Three hundred pounds of muscle and flesh. It moves with the speed of a bullet.

There is a strange, whistling noise as the creature aims for the diver's head. Closer and closer it comes. Fifteen inches from

Inside the mouth are 200 sharp, deadly teeth.

A FRIEND IN THE SEA

the man's face, the speeding form brakes to a full stop.

Its huge mouth opens. Inside are nearly 200 sharp, deadly teeth. Is a horrible deep-sea death about to take place?

No. Instead, the diver's face suddenly breaks into a broad smile. "Good boy, Tuffy," he says. He gives the huge creature a friendly pat.

What is this "terrible creature"? A trained dolphin, no less. "Tuffy" is a name this dolphin won for its many battles with sharks.

Tuffy and the diver are partners in a training program for the U.S. Navy. Tuffy has just proved how dolphins can save men lost in the ocean.

A little more than a minute after hearing the buzzer, Tuffy had made two dives. First he dived down to the submarine. A guideline was tied to his body. Then he raced toward the "lost" diver, bringing

Tuffy is rewarded for doing a good job.

A FRIEND IN THE SEA

him the lifesaving line.

How was Tuffy able to find the diver? Tuffy made use of the special hearing dolphins have. As they swim through the water, dolphins make noises—whistles, sighs, squeaks, cries. They sound playful. But dolphins make good use of these noises.

They listen for the echoes that their noises make. From the echoes, dolphins can pretty well tell the size, direction, and distance of objects that are far away.

Scientists have been learning more and more about dolphins. The experiment with Tuffy is just one of many.

Doris is the name of another dolphin scientists have been studying. One day her trainer cut a tiny pill in half. He hid it on the bottom of Doris' big swimming tank. Doris found the half-pill without a bit of trouble just by using her sense of hearing. The half-pill gave off tiny fizzing sounds.

In other tests, Doris was able to tell a

Dolphins have proved, in all their experiments, that they are smarter than most other animals.

toy fish from a real fish at a long distance. She could tell the difference between two kinds of metals. She could swim through difficult passages and not get lost. And she did all these things by the echoes that came back to her.

But how do we know that Doris did these things with hearing alone? In all her experiments Doris was blindfolded.

It seems clear that dolphins are smart, much smarter than most other animals. And, in addition, dolphins seem to like people and want to please them too.

Once, a fisherman opened Tuffy's pen and let him out into the open ocean. He was free to swim away and never return. But Tuffy came back on his trainer's signal.

Dolphins like Tuffy are big and powerful. Their teeth could easily bite a man's arm off. Yet dolphins will not harm a human being, even in self-defense. Many times, harpooned dolphins have refused to

THE BLOOD SUCKERS

strike back at the people who were hurting them.

Some scientists believe that dolphins would make fine lifeguards. They would be especially helpful in waters where there are sharks. Dolphins and sharks are deadly enemies.

A Florida woman told this real-life story:

"I went out waist-deep in the ocean. Suddenly I was swept off my feet by a huge wave. I swallowed a lot of water and couldn't get up. I knew that I'd never make it unless someone saved me.

"All at once, something gave me a tremendous push. I landed on the beach, facedown, too tired to turn over.

"A man who had seen this from a distance came running over. He said a dolphin was trying to protect me from a shark that was also swimming nearby."

Other people have told similar stories

Some scientists believe that dolphins would make fine lifeguards.

THE BLOOD SUCKERS

about being saved by dolphins from drowning or from sharks. These stories are not hard to believe. Dolphins often help each other in the same way.

Dolphins, like their larger cousins, the whales, can't breathe underwater. Right after birth, a baby dolphin must swim to the surface of the water to take its first breath. The mother watches carefully.

If the baby is weak, the mother helps lift it to the surface. Even when a dolphin calf is born dead, the mother does not give up. She pushes her dead baby to the surface. Sometimes she carries the dead baby on her back for days before giving up hope.

In the same way, dolphins help one another stay afloat when they are wounded or sick. Once, a dolphin was knocked out as it was being moved into a new tank. Right away two other dolphins in the tank swam over to help. They put their heads under the injured dolphin's flippers. Then

the surface of the water to take its first breath.

THE BLOOD SUCKERS

they held her on the surface of the water until she came to.

Some people think dolphins have other reasons for their strange, underwater noises. Reasons beside finding things. These people believe dolphins talk to each other. They think that people can learn to talk to them. If true, that's an exciting idea.

Maybe dolphins could help us understand the secrets of the ocean. Perhaps they could lead us to underwater wonders that no man has ever seen before.

We are just beginning to know the dolphin. In many ways, he seems almost like man. He loves games. He gets unhappy when he's kept away from his loved ones. He gets sick when life gets too hard for him.

A dolphin in Florida even likes to watch TV. One day the dolphin's trainers lowered a TV set into the dolphin's tank. Soon the dolphin began acting strangely.

A FRIEND IN THE SEA

He "talked" loudly, swam rapidly around his tank, and threw his ball high in the air again and again. Was he going crazy or something? Worried, his trainers went to see what was wrong.

When they saw what was happening, they started laughing. No wonder! The dolphin had been watching a baseball game on TV. But watching wasn't enough for him. Like his friend, man, the dolphin had to play all the positions too.

The Uncrowned King

By Diane Carlson

The travelers were riding through one of Africa's national parks. It was a peaceful place. An elephant was eating grass by the side of the road. He looked so friendly that the driver stopped the car and got out. He offered the gentle giant a breakfast roll.

But the elephant was more interested in the man than the roll. He grabbed the man

THE UNCROWNED KING

with his trunk and tossed him 20 feet into the air. Then the elephant knelt on the poor fellow.

Imagine having two cars piled on top of you. That's how much the elephant weighed. The man was crushed into powder.

The other people in the car got out and ran away as fast as they could. The elephant could easily have caught them, too, if he tried. He can walk faster than the fastest man can run.

Luckily, for the crushed man's friends, the elephant became interested in the car. With his trunk, his heavy tusks, and his huge feet, he smashed it into a twisted heap of junk.

The lion is known as the king of beasts. But some people think the crown really belongs to the elephant. He is the largest land animal in the world. Most elephants are twice as tall as a man. The elephant's

THE BLOOD SUCKERS

7-foot-long ivory tusks stick out of his jaws like giant teeth. His powerful trunk can pull down a concrete wall. Yet that same trunk can gently lift a tiny peanut from a glass-topped table without damaging the table.

No other animal except man is a match for the elephant. And man, of course, has weapons to help him out. Even with his weapons, a man may have a hard time bringing the great beast down. Hundreds of bullets have sometimes been poured into a single elephant before he falls.

Usually, this king is a peaceful ruler. He eats nothing but plants. In fact, that's how he spends most of his time — eating. An elephant eats about a thousand pounds of grass, leaves, bark, and vegetables every day. Twenty-two out of every 24 hours is spent eating.

Since he does not eat meat, an elephant does not kill other animals for food. He

Twenty-two out of every 24 hours is spent eating.

THE BLOOD SUCKERS

doesn't kill for the fun of it either. But when he does fight, watch out.

Sometimes a hungry lion will attack a newborn elephant. Unless that lion can run fast, he will not live to try it again. The baby's mother may pick the lion up, smash it against the trees, sit on it, stomp on its head, and pull its legs off one by one. That's her way of saying "Don't mess around with my kids."

Over the years, the elephant has been a much better friend to man than the other way around. The elephant is the most important work animal in many parts of the world—even today.

What makes elephants act as the one that killed the man with the breakfast roll did? Probably the cruel way elephants have been treated by man. Elephants have been teased, tortured, and shot at by human beings for thousands of years.

Two thousand years ago, the Romans

Over the years, the elephant has been a much better friend to man than the other way around.

THE BLOOD SUCKERS

held a kind of show that thousands of people went to. They called these shows *circuses*. But a Roman circus was not like a circus as we know it today. At their circuses, the Romans tortured and murdered men and animals alike. They did this just for the fun of pleasing the people. They thought of it as a good show—like going to the movies.

At these shows, wild animals and people were placed in the ring together to kill one another. The circus customers were unhappy if many performers came out alive.

Elephants usually played a big part in these shows. Sometimes one man, armed with a sword, would fight an elephant. Sometimes 500 lions and leopards would fight against 30 elephants. Other times 500 men on horseback would fight against 20 elephants, each with three men on its back. The circus managers sometimes just let loose a mixed bag of elephants, lions,

Sometimes 500 lions and leopards would fight against 30 elephants.

THE BLOOD SUCKERS

crocodiles, bulls, and unarmed people in one big bloodbath.

Circuses today are entirely different. But elephants still play a big part in circuses. They lead the parades; they dance; they ride bicycles, juggle, dress up in funny clothes and pretend they are drunk.

This may not be anything new for some elephants. They seem to enjoy getting drunk in the wilds. They know what the stuff is that will get them drunk, too — the ripe fruit of the *umganu* tree. Sometimes whole herds of elephants will stuff themselves with the fruit and stagger around in a daze. People who live where there are both elephants and umganu trees worry a lot when the fruit is ripe. An elephant can do a lot of damage when he is drunk.

One elephant in Africa had somehow gotten a taste for beer. One day he visited a place where beer was made. It was at a camp in an African national park.

THE UNCROWNED KING

Sometimes whole herds of elephants will stuff themselves with the fruit and stagger around in a daze.

THE BLOOD SUCKERS

The elephant lifted the roof right off the building where the beer was made. He leaned against nearby houses and pushed them in. He had to be shot after he picked up a car with people inside it and turned it upside down.

An elephant must be treated with great care. Farmers, zoo keepers, circus handlers, and hunters all say that even a friendly elephant can be dangerous — even when he doesn't want to be. Often he doesn't know his own strength. You have only to see a working elephant pull a full-grown tree out of the ground to know what they mean.

The Animal That Broke All the Rules

By Steven Otfinoski

It all started in 1797 in the backwoods of southern Australia. A man had trapped a small animal. It was the strangest animal anyone had ever seen.

It was covered with brown fur and had a flattened tail. Its four feet were webbed like a duck's. Instead of a mouth, it had the bill of a bird.

THE BLOOD SUCKERS

The man had found the animal digging a hole by the water's edge. For this reason, he called it a water-mole.

After the animal died, its skin was shipped to London, England. There many scientists studied it. Some of them called the skin a fake. They said no such animal ever lived. Someone had sewn a duck's bill and feet onto the skin of a beaver. That's what they said anyway.

But one man, Dr. Irving Shaw, said the skin was real. Dr. Shaw called this new animal a *platypus*. The word meant a flat-footed animal with a duckbill. The animal is still known by this name today.

But the new animal needed more than a name. It had to be listed like all the other known animals.

The three lists of animals at that time were *mammals,* *birds,* and *reptiles.* All mammals were warm-blooded and had hair on their bodies, scientists said. They

They claimed no such animal ever existed.

THE BLOOD SUCKERS

gave birth to their young live. They didn't hatch them out of eggs. They also had teeth, four limbs and two ears. Horses, dogs, and apes are examples of mammals. Dr. Shaw felt the platypus belonged on the list of mammals.

Suddenly a strange discovery was made. A platypus nest was uncovered. Eggs were found in it. Did this mean the platypus wasn't a mammal after all?

Some scientists refused to believe that the eggs were laid by a platypus. They claimed the eggs were really turtle eggs put in the nest as a trick. The argument about the eggs went on for years.

Then in 1832 an English scientist went to Australia. He uncovered dozens of platypus nests. He found platypuses of all ages. He saw mother platypuses feeding their young milk. But he found no eggs.

Fifty years later the mystery was solved. It happened quite by accident. Another

Suddenly a platypus nest was uncovered.

THE BLOOD SUCKERS

English scientist was studying a female platypus. He opened her pouch; and, to his surprise, he found an egg inside.

"So that's why no one could find the eggs!" he said. "The animal keeps them in her pouch."

He also discovered another interesting fact. All mammals are warm-blooded animals, while reptiles, like snakes and lizards, are cold-blooded. The platypus was warm-blooded too. But its blood was colder than all other mammals'. *Did this mean that the platypus was a cross between mammal and reptile?* scientists asked themselves. They finally decided there was only one explanation.

The platypus goes back to a time when reptiles were slowly changing into mammals on the earth. This probably took place many thousands of years ago.

The platypus would have disappeared long ago if Australia were not so cut off

He opened her pouch and found an egg inside.

THE BLOOD SUCKERS

from the rest of the world. Australia is a large island that had very few people living on it until recently. There was no one around to kill off the platypus. It cannot be found anywhere else in the world today, except in zoos.

We now know quite a lot about the platypus. We know it eats insects, worms, and small shellfish. One platypus in a zoo ate 40 shrimp, 40 bugs and half a pound of earthworms in one day!

Back in 1882, the English scientist had discovered that the female platypus puts its eggs in a pouch. But he didn't know that she doesn't keep them there the whole time. About ten days before the eggs are ready to hatch, the female crawls into a special hole and builds herself a nest for the eggs. She makes the nest out of leaves soaked in water. Then sits on the eggs until they hatch.

The baby platypuses are blind for the

THE ANIMAL THAT BROKE—

The female sits on the eggs until they hatch.

THE BLOOD SUCKERS

first three months of life. They live on their mother's milk for nearly half a year. After that, they must learn how to get food for themselves.

The platypus can fight when it has to. All males have a spur on their hind legs. They can wound their enemies with this spur. The wound is like the bite of a rattlesnake, but not as deadly. One man who was hit on his hand by the spur could not move his hand for nine weeks.

What the spur really does is still a mystery. Some scientists believe it puts a drug into the blood of the victim. The drug slows the victim down, they say.

Another mystery is the strange beak of the platypus. It is soft and rubbery and looks just like a duck's beak. Why is it there and what is it used for? One explanation is that the platypus "feels" its way around in the water with its beak when its eyes and ears are shut. Another

THE ANIMAL THAT BROKE—

explanation is that the platypus uses the beak like a shovel to dig with.

The platypus may be among the lowest of mammals. But the highest mammal—man—hasn't figured him out yet!

The Deadliest of Them All

By Diane Carlson

In World War II many ships were sunk and planes were shot down at sea. Helpless pilots and sailors fell into the water. Some had life jackets. Some just had parts of the wreck to hold on to. Many were wounded and bleeding. They were an easy target for sharks!

No one knows how many soldiers and

THE DEADLIEST OF THEM ALL

sailors lost their lives to sharks during the war. Some men lived through such attacks. Navy Commander Keith Kabat was one of these men. Kabat's ship was sunk by the Japanese in the Pacific Ocean in May 1944. Here is his story:

"When the bombs fell," Kabat said, "I just had time to get into my life jacket. I had no shoes on when I went into the water. Suddenly my left foot felt like something was tickling it. I held up my foot. It was bleeding.

"I looked into the water. Not 10 feet away I saw the brown back of a big fish swimming away from me. The real fear did not hit me until I saw him turn and head back toward me. He didn't rush but came in a steady direct line. I kicked and splashed and this time he turned away and went back to swimming in a circle around me.

"Then he came at me again. When he

The shark came at him again and again.

THE DEADLIEST OF THEM ALL

was almost upon me. I brought my fist down on his nose again and again. He swam off again. I found a piece of my left hand gone. Again he struck. This time the flesh was torn from my left arm. The big toe on my left foot was gone and a piece of my right heel. His rough hide scraped my skin raw."

Kabat saw a ship. He waved and shouted for help. The shark struck again, biting Kabat's hip down to the bone. Men on the ship saw Kabat and shot the shark. Kabat was saved. He was in a hospital many months, but his wounds finally healed.

Stories like this make some people think sharks would rather eat humans than anything else. But this isn't true. If it were, many sharks would starve to death. There are just not enough people in the sea to feed them.

Each year about 30 people are attacked

Dying in the jaws of a powerful shark is the worst thing a lot of people can think of.

THE DEADLIEST OF THEM ALL

by sharks all over the world. Half these people die. That's not very many though. More swimmers are struck by lightning each year than are killed by sharks. But dying in the jaws of a powerful shark is the worst thing a lot of people can think of.

Of the 250 different kinds of sharks, only 24 will attack man. It is not easy to tell which sharks are dangerous and which are not. The best way to tell is by the sharks' teeth. Man-eaters have saw-edged teeth. Other sharks have flat teeth. But who wants to get close enough to find out?

The early Romans had an answer. A horrible one. When a shark was seen where people were swimming, everybody was ordered out of the water. Then a slave was picked up and thrown in the water. If the slave was not hurt, they knew the shark was harmless. The people could go on swimming. If the shark attacked the slave, the people stayed out.

THE BLOOD SUCKERS

Size is not a good way to tell whether a shark is dangerous. The biggest shark of all is the whale shark. Whale sharks grow up to 60 feet long. That's the lenght of ten men placed in a line head to toe. Yet whale sharks eat only tiny water plants and animals that you can hardly see. Divers have been known to hitch rides on the backs of whale sharks. The beasts don't seem to mind at all.

But some small sharks can be deadly. Not long ago a fisherman in Florida hooked a 4-foot shark. The fisherman pulled on his line. Finally he got the fish next to his boat. Then he leaned over. He tried to lift it into the boat by the tail. In a flash, the beast turned around and bit off the fisherman's hand. It then jumped back into the water, broke the line and swam away. The fisherman's hand was still in its mouth.

Sharks can smell a small amount of

THE DEADLIEST OF THEM ALL

The shark swam away, the fisherman's hand still in its mouth.

THE BLOOD SUCKERS

blood in the water from far away. Blood excites a shark. It tells him food is nearby.

A hunting shark can find where the smell is coming from by rolling its body from side to side. It sniffs the water on one side, then the other, as it follows the trail.

During a kill, sharks get so excited that even a shark may get bitten. Then the other sharks turn on the injured shark and tear it to pieces. The smell and taste of blood drives sharks wild.

Sharks are not fussy eaters though. They love blood, but they will eat almost anything. If there's nothing around to eat, a shark can live off the fat in its liver for up to two months.

Just about anything can end up in a shark's stomach. When sharks have been killed and their stomachs cut open, men have found all kinds of junk inside. Beer bottles. Maps. Parts of toys. Pieces of wood. Rusty nails.

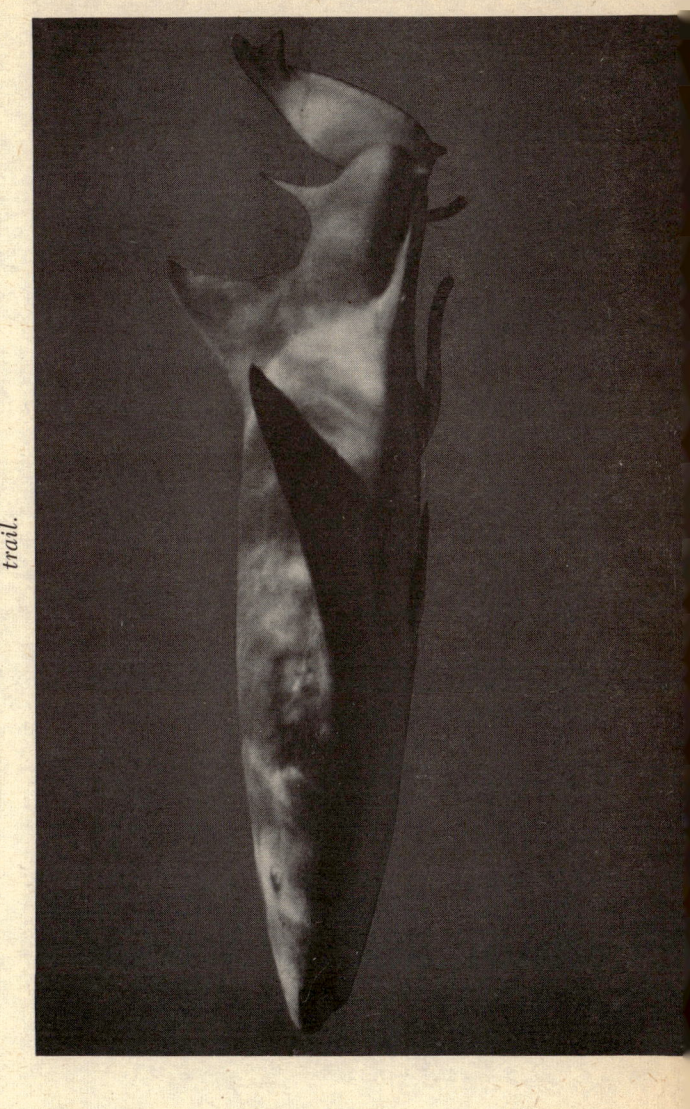

A hunting shark snaps the water as it follows the trail.

THE BLOOD SUCKERS

Don't these hard objects give the shark a stomachache? If they do, he has a way of getting rid of them. He turns his stomach inside out and forces it through his mouth into the water. The sea water washes out the unwanted objects. The stomach then slides back into place. It is like turning a pocket inside out to empty it.

Scientists are trying to find a simple way to keep sharks from attacking people in the water. So far no one has found anything that works all the time.

The United States Navy has a new way to protect pilots or sailors lost at sea. Tough plastic bags are folded into a package. These are attached to the man's life jacket. The bag is a little bigger than a man. The man gets into the bag after the life jacket is blown up. The bag hangs down from the life jacket. Sharks cannot see the man's feet hanging in the water. If he is bleeding, the bag is even more im-

THE DEADLIEST OF THEM ALL

The bag hangs down from the life jacket and protects the man's body.

THE BLOOD SUCKERS

portant. The bag holds his blood inside so a shark will not smell it and attack.

People on islands of the Pacific Ocean have learned to live with sharks. They have to. Over half their food comes from the sea. Parents teach children at an early age about sharks. Several sharks are caught and placed in shallow pools where the children play. The sharks can't get away. And they cannot swim as fast here as they can in deep water.

The children learn how to stay out of a shark's way. They also learn not to be afraid of sharks. When the children are old enough to fish underwater, they will not panic when they see a shark. They have learned to be careful.

The Price of Honey

By Diane Carlson

Imagine a city of 30,000 people. In this city the men lie around all day and take it easy. They never work—none of them. They don't even feed themselves. When they open their mouths, women come around and drop the food in.

It's a different story for the women in this city. All they do is work. Twenty-four

THE BLOOD SUCKERS

hours a day. They never sleep. They never play. If they are not building houses, they are out getting food. If they aren't taking care of the children, they are sweeping the streets. They even make up the police force. And they are tough cops. When a stranger shows up in town, they kill him.

It's a great place to be a man. Except for one thing. Every once in a while, the women get fed up with doing all the work. Then they take the men to the edge of the city and kick them out. It is winter. The men have never learned to do anything for themselves. If they don't starve to death, some mugger comes along and hits them over the head.

But don't think the women in this city have the last laugh. At least the men have had an easy life before they die. The women work themselves to death. All of them.

This is a true story. Only it is really

THE PRICE OF HONEY

about bees instead of people.

Male honeybees are lazy bums like the men in our story. They buzz and stumble around the hive, waiting to be fed. They can't even protect themselves. If you are ever stung by a honeybee, you can be sure the bee was female. Male honeybees don't have stingers.

Female honeybees put up with the males for only one reason. They need the males for mating purposes. Without two sexes, there can't be any little bees. But only one female in the hive has any children—the queen.

The queen bee isn't a queen like other queens. She doesn't take it easy or order the other bees around. Her special job is laying the eggs that will hatch into new bees. She is almost an egg-laying machine. All summer long she lays about two eggs a minute 24 hours a day.

Even though she is the queen, she had

better do her job right. If the workers see that she is slowing up, they kick her out of the hive or sting her to death. This is also what happens to the helpless males after the queen has been mated. They are pushed out of the hive. They soon starve to death or get killed by larger insects.

It is the workers who make new queens. The queen bee lays both male and female eggs. None of the eggs contain queens to start out with. The workers give some of the female eggs a special food. People call this food *royal jelly* because it has the power to turn plain females into royal queens.

But there can be only one queen in every hive. When the old queen isn't laying eggs, she spends her time breaking open any queen eggs she sees. Then she kills the little bees inside.

Every once in a while, though, she misses an egg. And another queen hatches.

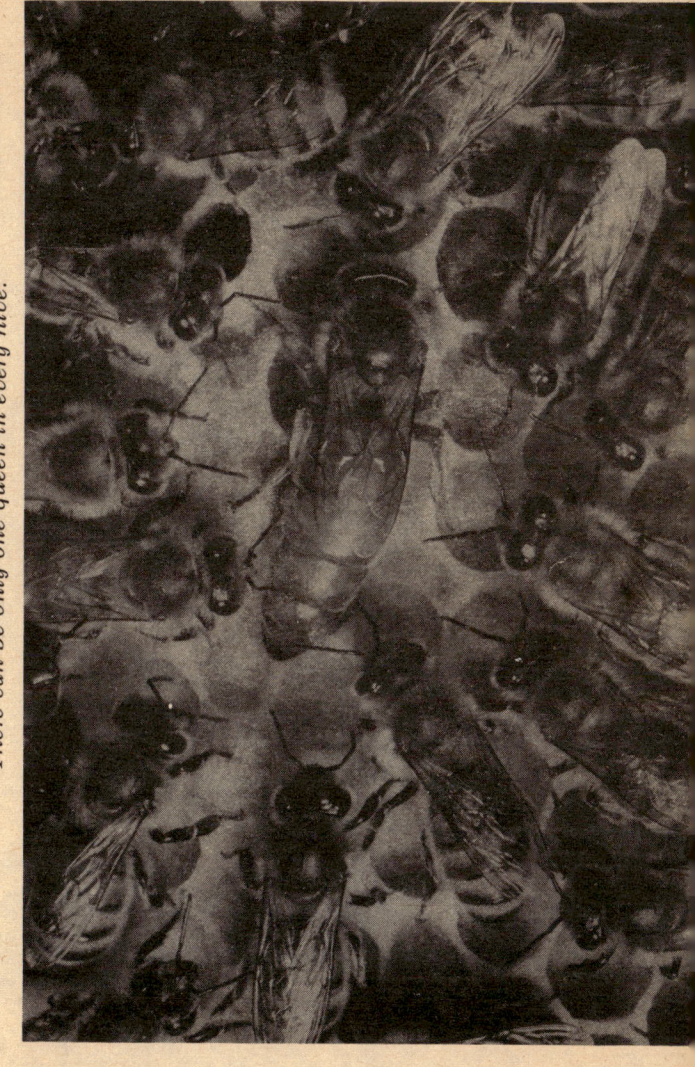

There can be only one queen in every hive.

THE BLOOD SUCKERS

Then it is a battle to the death between the two queens. The workers stand around and watch. They don't care if mother kills daughter or daughter kills mother — just so long as there is one queen left to lay eggs.

Bees have tiny brains. This is hard to believe when you look at some of the things bees do. For example, some bees guard the doors of the hive to keep strange bees out. Once in a while, a larger creature, like a mouse, sneaks into the hive. The guards attack and sting it to death, even though it is many times their size.

But then comes the problem of getting the dead monster out of the hive. A whole bunch of bees may get together and try to push it out. If this doesn't work, the bees make wax inside their bodies. Then they seal up the dead mouse in the wax. The wax keeps the dead body from rotting and smelling up the place.

Maybe the most amazing thing of all is

Once in a while, a mouse sneaks into the hive.
The guards attack and sting it to death.

THE BLOOD SUCKERS

the way bees can tell one another where to find a good field of flowers. Honey is made from the juices that bees collect from flowers. Flying from flower to flower, bees travel about 50,000 miles to make one pound of honey. That's like making two complete trips around the world.

When a bee finds an especially good field of flowers, she flies back to the hive. Then she does a dance to tell the rest of the workers where it is. The way the bee dances tells the others exactly how far to fly and in which direction.

Bees do the same kind of dance if they have seen a good place for a new home.

A German scientist named Otto von Frisch figured out what the steps in the bee-dance meant. He would watch a bee do her dance. Then he would go as fast as he could to the place he thought she was telling about. Soon after he got there, a whole bunch of bees would come along.

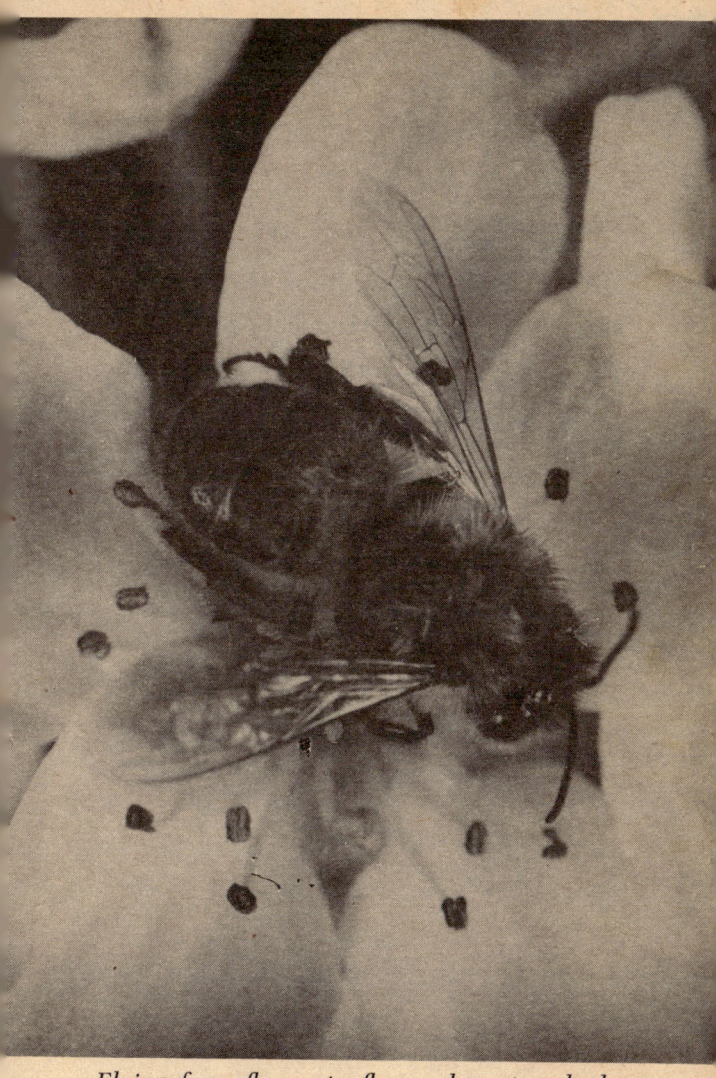

Flying from flower to flower, bees travel about 50,000 miles to make one pound of honey.

THE BLOOD SUCKERS

Von Frisch was a teacher. One day he and some of his students were watching some bees who seemed very excited. Von Frisch gave the students the same directions that the bees were giving to each other.

The students hopped on their bicycles and rode as fast as they could go. The directions took them right into the center of a city. They stopped at an outdoor cafe. People were having lunch at tables set up on the sidewalk.

The students started arguing among themselves. "Von Frisch must be wrong," one of them said. "Why would the bees come here?"

The owner of the cafe came out and asked the young men what they were doing.

"Waiting for the bees," one said.

"What's the joke?" the owner said.

Just then the bees arrived. Thousands of

The students hopped on their bicycles and rode to an outdoor cafe.

them. They had come to build a new hive in a hollow tree nearby. The people sitting in the cafe were in a panic. Men and women screamed. They knocked over dishes and tables in their rush to get away from the bees.

The cafe owner called the police. "Some guys are down here trying to wreck my business," he said. "I don't know how they did it, but they brought a million bees with them."

The police arrested the students. Von Frisch himself had to come down and explain the whole thing. He told the police how bees can talk to one another by dancing. He told them how he had learned to understand their language.

"But a bee is only an insect," said one policeman. "How can it do all these things?"

Von Frisch only shook his head. "That's the part I haven't figured out yet," he said.

Wolf on the Run

By Steven Otfinoski

When you hear the word *wolf* what do you think of? Probably a dangerous animal! Maybe you hear howling at night on the open prairie and see a few men huddled around a campfire. Their guns are ready for the wolf attack.

Well, that may be the way it is in the movies. But in real life, wolves aren't all

THE BLOOD SUCKERS

that bad. Wolves are actually wild dogs. In some ways wolves are like people. They live in family groups and often stay with the same mate for life. Few other animals do this.

Members of the same wolf family live together, hunt together, and are very good friends. If a wolf outside the family circle tries to join them, however, they will chase him away. If he doesn't leave quietly, they will kill him. When a female wolf gives birth, everyone in the family helps take care of the pups. The females must like that!

True wolves are not troublemakers. They keep to themselves and stay away from people. Most of them are afraid of men. Then why do men hate wolves so? Why do wolves have a bad name? Very often because in this country, at least, wolves are mistaken for coyotes.

This is certainly the problem facing the

Wolves are actually wild dogs.

THE BLOOD SUCKERS

red wolf who lives in the southern and western parts of the United States. He gets blamed for what the coyote does, and the mistake is costing him his life.

The trouble is, the coyote likes to travel near farms and raid barnyards for hens and other farm animals. Naturally this doesn't go over very big with the farmers. And who do they blame? The wolf!

Are the red wolf and the coyote all that much alike? Not really. The red wolf's natural home is the forest and brush. The coyote's natural home is the open plain, prairie, and desert.

The coyote is about the same color as the red wolf. But the red wolf is larger in size and has rougher fur.

There are lots of other differences. So why the mix-up between the two animals? For one thing, the farther west you go, the smaller the red wolf becomes. Then it is harder to tell the red wolf from the coyote.

The coyote is about the same color as the red wolf, but smaller.

THE BLOOD SUCKERS

People who see a pack of coyotes often mistake it for a pack of wolves. They think there are thousands of red wolves running wild. Then they begin to hunt and shoot them.

The fight to prove the red wolf is a wolf and not a coyote is an interesting one. It went on for many years. Even scientists took part. One team of scientists proved the difference in the 1960's by using tape recordings of wolf howls in the wild.

The tape-recorded howls were played in the forest at night. Wolves, coyotes, and dogs answered the recorded howls. Each animal had a different howl.

The coyote's howl was short and high-pitched. The wolf's howl was lower and longer. The dog's howl was like the wolf's. However, the dogs barked a lot as they howled. The wolf only barks when he's in serious danger. These days it seems the red wolf has plenty to bark about.

WOLF ON THE RUN

The wolf only barks when he's in serious danger.

THE BLOOD SUCKERS

Red wolves have been disappearing from their home grounds for some years. Few people know it, however. Forests have been torn down for housing and other building purposes. The red wolf is not a fighter, so he retreats to the little forest area left to him. The coyote *is* a fighter. He can change with the times. Because of this, coyotes have grown in number.

In the state of Louisiana, people were afraid the red wolf was getting out of hand. So hunters killed off many of them. Soon nearly all the red wolves were gone. The balance of nature was thrown off. There was no predator to control the number of other animals in the state. A predator is an animal that hunts and eats other animals.

The coyote is a predator like the red wolf. He came into Louisiana after the red wolf had almost disappeared. With the red wolf gone, there were many animals to hunt and eat. The coyote did more damage

The coyote did more damage to farms than the red wolf.

to farms than the red wolf ever did. He was harder for trappers and hunters to catch and kill, too.

Louisiana learned its lesson. But it was too late to save the red wolf in that state.

Is anything being done to save the red wolves that are still left in other places? The answer is yes. The Fish and Wildlife Service wants land that's suitable for the red wolf to be added to wildlife refuges. A refuge is an area of land set aside for animals in danger of being completely wiped out. On a refuge these animals are protected by law from hunters and other dangers.

One problem in setting aside a refuge for red wolves is space. A pack of red wolves will roam over an area from 50 to 100 square miles. A normal refuge would be too small for them. They would wander outside it all the time.

People who want to save the red wolf

say that any coyotes found inside the refuges should be killed. This way the red wolf won't have to fight for his food. Some farm animals in the area may be killed by the wolves, these people say. But instead of killing the wolves, they think the Government should pay the farmers for their lost animals.

Most important of all, hunters should be taught to think of the wolf as another living thing. That's most important of all, these people say.

While refuges are being set up, it's possible to raise red wolves in zoos. There are five zoos today in the west that are caring for red wolves.

But time is running out. There were three kinds of red wolves. One kind lived in Florida. It has not been seen since the early 1940's. One kind lived along the Mississippi River. It is almost all gone, too. The third kind can still be found in some of the western states. But, something must be done soon to save the red wolf. Otherwise he will soon be gone. There is no place left for him to run. Time is running out.